"Someday I'll be a weather-beaten skull
resting on a grass pillow,
serenaded by a stray bird or two.
Kings and commoners end up the same,
no more enduring than last night's dream."

~ *Ryōkan*

Musing
on the
Cricket Game
of Life
Part One and a Half

by
James E. Roéthlein

Box # 5 – 720 Sixth Street
New Westminster BC
CANADA V3L3C5

Title: "Musing on the Cricket Game of Life One and a Half"
Author: James E. Roéthlein
Layout: Candice James

ISBN 978-1-927616-88-8 Softcover book
ISBN 978-1-927616-89-5 Electronic book

Library and Archives Canada Cataloguing in Publication

Roéthlein, James E., 1971-, author
        Musing on the cricket game of life : part one and
a half / by James E. Roéthlein.

Poems.
Includes index.
Issued in print and electronic formats.
ISBN 978-1-927616-88-8 (softcover).--ISBN 978-1-927616-89-5
(PDF)

        I. Title.

PS3618.039M87 2018   811'.6   C2018-904751-8

                                                    C2018-904752-6

Acknowledgements

I would like to thank my Lord and Savior for the gift of poetry, to the Wordsmythes: Gene, Mike E., Mike Z., Daniel, Matt, and Bob. I would also like to thank my fellow poets from World Poetry Open Mic., both you and the Wordsmythes have been there to encourage me and to help me improve my poetry, many thanks.

~ James E. Roéthlein

Author's Note: The following publications have published my work

The Sheltered Poet
When She First Knew a Man, The Flower-Scented Air and Poets

MagnaPoets
The Harrowing of Hell *originally titled Prisoner of War*

Speedpoets
This not a Poem about the Rain and Experiencing the Other Name for Autumn.

New Thoreau Quarterly
After a Storm, Spring 1987

World Poetry Open Mic Anthology 2016
After a Storm, Spring 1987, Mrs. Hughes Has Died, Phather Phantasm, and Wildflower

World Poetry Open Mic Anthology 2017
The Harrowing of Hell, The Flower-Scented Air,

Honeysuckle
Love Letter from a Minefield

Ceremony
Mrs. Hughes Has Died

Helix Magazine
Murder of the First Degree

Poet's Haven Digest: Darker Than Fiction
Shrouded in Fog Beneath the Gaslight

Table of Contents

Ode to the New Modern Man

I stand in awe
of the demasculinized man,
enduring decades under the knife
of systematic societal surgery.

A word here, a notion there,
he emerges mentally emasculated,
deemed worthy to bring progeny into the world
and little more,
leaving the strong women (whom we need) alone
to bear the burden of rearing a generation.

So, raise a glass
to the men we've molded,
and celebrate the creeping chaos
that comes from their making,
which we call progress.

After a Storm, Spring 1987

Rainclouds retreating in the distance,
leaving the world outside my window,
peaceful in its wake.

And I wonder,
is this what it was like in London,
when the dust settled
after the final German rocket fell?

Experiencing the Other Name for Autumn

Gravity is the attraction of a smaller body to a larger one,
and standing high upon a ladder, I was attracted to the
Earth.
With arms flailing, I soared with ease through the empty air,
perpetrating, yet another horrendous bird imitation.

Perhaps, if I were descending from a loftier height
I could have contemplated the complexities
of constitutional law
or why my cats were regarding me with a disinterested air.

But as my journey downward was just a second long,
I (being allergic to pain), only had time to think,
of how much it would hurt, when I made that sudden stop.

The Harrowing of Hell

"... he descended into hell,
on the third day, he rose again from the dead..."
-Apostles' Creed

Broken sword and shattered shield,
he lay there fallen upon the field.
The prisoner of war carried away,
to the realm where the enemy held sway.
Held captive in Mephistopheles' Hall,
fettered and chained, for the amusement of all.
Midst the celebration of his defeat,
he broke the bonds holding his hands and feet.
Striding forth with a triumphant shout,
he broke the gates of Hell, from the inside out.

This is not a Poem about the Rain

This is not a poem about the rain
insomuch as to what the rain is doing,
but rather a poem about what it is not,
and what is not,
is coming down handsomely; somewhere else.
It is also not coming down on a day other than Monday,
which as it happens is today,
so, I know I'll be twice as depressed

My two cats, who care nothing
for what the rain is not doing,
are regarding me as they always do:
as their scratching post, chew toy,
the bringer of their food;
and due to the liquid nature of the weather,
I'm cooped up with them on my day off,
waiting for the rain to do,
what it is not.

Poets

We the music makers and dreamers of dreams *
keep a sleepless vigil
in the lonely watches of the night.
Pacing the floor
in the silent realm of our room
we give voice to the inexpressible thought,
speaking of patients etherized upon a table **
and how she bowed to her brother, ***
of Daddy ****;
of crystal stairs *****
and the road not taken ******.

The world may sleep soundly tonight,
knowing that a poet is wide awake.
For it is said the world will end,
when the last poet awake, falls asleep.

* Ode – Arthur O' Shaughnessy
** The Love Song of J. Alfred Prufrock -T.S. Eliot
*** She Bowed to Her Brother- Gertrude Stein
**** Daddy -Sylvia Plath
***** Mother to Son -Langston Hughes
****** The Road Not Taken – Robert Frost

Mrs. Hughes Has Died

Mrs. Hughes has died
in the lonely watches of the night,
her body in celebrated repose.

And the ravenous wolves
gathered at her tomb,
caring only for the scent
of her lovely bones,
gave no thought of who she was
and how she lived.

Wildflower

She is the wildflower,
golden and lovely,
blooming in the garden of his delight;
her meadowed charms have softened his stone heart,
ashen, from years wandering the wastelands,
stumbling on the rocks of unrequited love.

The Flower-Scented Air

The flower-scented air
masks a road of broken glass and thorn,
and I, the fool,
walked it barefoot for miles,
unwilling to take a safer road,
for fear of the pain of repentance.

Phather Phantasm

Half-seen in my half-stare,
half-believing you are there.

Faded memories and faded thoughts,
raindrops falling on sun-seared rock,
quickly come, and quickly part.

I was eleven when you did not die;
you took your leave, never saying goodbye.

And I, the fool, follow the fool
walking barefoot on broken glass,
and tread upon the blood-stained shards,
waiting to wound me ere I pass.

He Closes His Eyes

He closes his eyes to hear her read,
the exterior of her form, nubile in his mind,
and a distraction
from the exquisite beauty of her verse.

The soft lilt of her voice
takes him to a place he'd never leave
if he stayed too long,
but if he shut his ears,
he'd be less for the missed experience.

His Soul Took Ship
(In memory of John Gordon)

His soul took ship,
over the sea,
to white shores and a green country
under a swift sunrise beyond.
Further up, and further in,
stepped thru the door
to the eternal side of time,
departing these shadowlands,
as Death, eager to claim another,
loses his lunch,
when the one he was there for,
came running with a grin.
And with the One who loved him,
dragged Death behind,
kicking, and screaming.

Portrait of Legacy

The portrait of my legacy,
yet unfinished, is painted
in dime-store aquarelle and fine oils;
and with brush in hand,
I add to the strokes already there.

The continental divide of my days
casts it's shadow upon me,
looming, either before me, or behind.
And as the twilight is descending
on all my days,
time will judge the mark I've made
when the portrait is on display.

The End of Advent

With the end of Advent
we rejoice;
a fifth candle to mark
the silent night shattered by praise,
as the darkness of the ages
was driven back by the Light.

With the end of Advent
we rejoice;
shepherds came, and shepherds saw
the lamb who would lead them,
and his mother
pondered these things in her heart.

With the end of Advent
we rejoice;
a star over India, guided west
the magicians to Judea,
and giving gifts to the kingly gift,
bowed low on bended knee.

With the end of Advent
we rejoice;
the middle cross on Golgotha's hill
marks the death-knell of all our sins,
and points us to Judah's lion
and the empty tomb he left behind.

I Stay Away

Raven haired beauty,
fair-skinned and tall,
the visage of perfection
I hold in my heart.

To hear her sweet voice
and be caught in her gaze,
I'd endure ev'ry peril
of the seven seas.

Alas, she will not have me,
for such is her wish.
And so, to honor her;
I stay away.

In Flights of Fancy

In flights of fancy
I yearn for her touch, her tender kiss.
The small dark cloud of a woman
with beautiful red flowing hair
holds me entranced,
captive to the power of her verse,
spoken years before
in her angelic voice of despair,
long since silenced by the grave.

In the Final Hours

27

My lengthening shadow
trails behind me, fleeing
the crepuscular light
in the waning moments
at the end of my day.

Alone in this hour
of obsidian night,
between what was, and what
shall be, I lay down, and
closing my eyes, I sleep.

When She First Knew a Man

A sigh
for her husband,
moaning, as he knew her,
her wide eyes, silently asking,
for more.

These Deadly Days

29

These deadly days, when
the innocent are slaughtered by the score,
gunned down in the hallway,
executed by the blackboard,
murdered in the womb;
As the blood of a generation
dries on our hands,
we slowly begin
not to care.

Love Letter from a Minefield

I.

I made love to you
as fire freezes water
and dead men still dream.

II.

Hand in bitter hand,
laughter-the slow twisting knife,
driving me away.

III.

Sullen stone-razor
wire crosses my wayward path
through these desert lands.

IV.

Loneliness whispered,
then I took her to my bed,
and thought it was love.

A Night in Virginia

Silence rules the realm
beneath the canvas veil;
sheltered from the howling wind
buffeting the world outside
in the lonely hours before dawn.

I lay there still
(the minstrels having bid goodbye),
my breath hanging like a fog
in the darkened air (from the thrice dead fire),
as others in similar realms,
slumber, in the arms of blissful dreams.

Lying Awake at 5 A.M.

32

Distant
siren's peeling;
shattered silence crowning
this quiet town,
and I begin to cry.

The Simpleton

The simpleton stands by the road,
    waving at cars
           waving at cars
                waving at cars,

moving more hearts,
than I ever could.

Dirge for the Quiet Man

Death
tip-toed
quietly for
the quiet man,
afraid to come,
lest he'd find him waiting.

Shrouded in Fog Beneath the Gaslight

35

Shrouded in fog beneath the gaslight,
a pale glow,
glinting on a knife in the dark;
and there, midst the gloom and shadow,
another life ebbs, flowing from the neck,
his dark deed, sight unseen,
and he walks away,
free to strike again in London,
shrouded in fog beneath the gaslight.

My Sister's Greenhouse

My sister's greenhouse is broken,
shattered by the one who shared it,
and the garden they grew,
torn in two,
poisoned with salt
as he left.

With the glass scattered on the ground
and the garden in disarray,
the God who watches and weeps,
is there beside her,
offering his healing hands.

Fog of War

The valiant and the victorious

A flash of fire and they died,
their blood hallowing the stained earth
where their broken bodies fell, and
the cries of wounded men mingled
with the smoke heavy in the air.

They lived to flee another day

They saw the elephant and ran,
leaving their brothers in the face
of advancing blue or grey;
their self-preservation, dearer
than duty, courage, and honor.

Black Masquerade

The grand illusion
of a so-called righteous life,
the citadel of my heart,
tainted to the core,
obsidian, in God's sight.

A Haiku Midst Pomp and Circumstance

*The child, not a child, advances
upon the calling of his name.*

The eagle takes flight

With tassel turned, and paper received,
they process to a larger world,

now ready to leave the nest

reveling in the end of the page,
and eager to see what the new chapter brings.

it will learn how to hunt

Before It's Too Late

The eagle has landed,
fallen with a thud.

Those among us mourning,
hold the smoking gun and bomb.

Our flag of freedom flutters
(midst gunshots and rhetoric)
slowly to the ground.

When words could heal and bind,
instead are used to draw and quarter.

Murder of the First Degree

It sounded like a
wet melon,
the splitting
of his "dear" brother's skull.

The State of Trees in St. Valentine's Forest

42

They saw
the oak had died
with half the other trees,
so, they chose not to plant one
of their own.

Silence and Shadow

Silence and shadow fill my room
at the end of yet another day
.
I sit there, staring at the four walls;
alone,
longing a hand to hold,
a woman's voice to hear.

After all these years,
        I still wait
        I still wait
        I still wait
to catch a glimpse of her.

A Thousand Fools

Speak to me,
voices from beyond.
Speak to me,
tell me what I wish to hear.

And a thousand fools
clamor to hear the siren's song
(thinking they can talk to the dead),
not caring they could die on the rocks
or wander in other such dangerous places.

Summer Savannah Stroll

The picture of a father,
walking hand in hand,
with his daughter and his son,
grows mightily in my mind,
imprinting itself on my soul.

I could describe to you,
the green foliage canopy overhead
and the cool breeze blowing through the trees
as they stroll towards the white marble fountain,
there at the end of a grey macadam road.

I suppose I could even mention
the conversation I imagine they're having
as the mother stands at a distance taking this picture.

But all this is a backdrop,
to what is really happening.

A father walking hand in hand
with his daughter and his son,
a rarity in these latter days.

The Mississippi Runs Red

Silence is in the air,
no voices carried on the wind
from sea to shining sea.

And the Mississippi runs red,
weeping with the bone-strewn land,
for our past sins and lack of vigilance.

The Strange Case of the Modern Man

Turmoil in the mind of modern man,
Henry and Edward vie for control
in the struggle of self since the Fall began.

And I,
being a man of the divided mind,
am one such battlefield.

Dear God in Heaven,
who but you,
can save me from myself?

It Gives Him Pause

She pretended to love him,
then she went away,
having as much affection for him
as would a dead cat.

But he was lonely
long before she left,
and when he said he loved her,
did he really feel it?

Second Coming

Standing majestic,
the mountain at the end of the road;
foreboding
to those who do not welcome the sight.

And though far closer,
than the prophets who first saw it,
I see little more
than the shape of its slopes,
shrouded, in the mists of future time.

Wild Wind

The wild wind ruling the waft and woods,
whistles thro' the trees
on the far side of the world
from where I stand.

Here on the oceans' edge,
the waters ask an age-old question
asked of Adam after he ate the apple,
"if you have no dominion over yourself,
how can you have dominion over me?"

Immortality

I.

She
died
slipping
eagerly
into Death's embrace.
The small dark cloud of a woman,
obeying the angelic voice of her deep despair.

II.

They
stand
huddled
at the grave.
Brother and sister
mourning the loss of their mother,
at an age, when they are far too young to understand.

III.

The
course
the years
have taken
has been kind to her.
In her last days, she made her name,
ensuring that Lady Lazarus will never die.

Picture Show

House lights dimming
in the darkened hall,
the patrons seated there, greeted
by discordant sights and sounds
assaulting their avant-garde senses,
found they liked the picture show.

Day of Destiny

I.

Weary,
needing release
from mediocre men
occupying the hallowed halls
of stone.

II.

Our cries
for better days
had fallen on the ears
of men who did not seem to hear
or care.

III.

So, we
chose from their ranks
the man who would be king,
believing he had come to bring
us hope.

IV.

Watching
us watching him,
he stood upon the stage,
his day of destiny had now
arrived.

He's That into Her

Staring
long at her pair,
ev'rytime she is near,
lost, in the sensuousness, of
her eyes.

One Day in the Court
Matt. 2:16

55

A callous heart,
with the notion it's convenient
to slaughter the undesired child,
wherever he may slumber.
So many years have passed
since that fateful day,
when the decree came from court,
and the innocent were put to the blade,
all to protect one person's way of life.

Precious. Little You
(for Aria)

The ceiling was split open,
and the veil was rolled away,
when you were brought forth
into this great wide world.

A wonder of wonders,
the miracle life begetting life,
designed by a loving God,
and manifested in the precious, little gift,
of precious, little you.

Why Must It Be So?

57

One little boy,
dead,
bloodied beyond compare.

One little boy,
laid,
in an open casket.

Many little boys,
dead,
before change could occur.

Flower Bearer

He came to us
(the land in need of peace)
with flowers in his hand,
when other kings had come,
bringing fire and the sword.

We met him on the road
and followed him into the city.

We cheered for him and sang to him,
but soon we began to mock him.
We beat him and bled him
and hung him out to die.

He looked on us and loved us,
as we looked on him and loathed him.

In a different time, a different place,
things would have remained the same.

The Wild Goose of the Ancient Days

White-hot fingers of flame,
lick the air, casting shadows on the sand.

The silent speaker comes,
stands beside me, whispers in my soul's ear

One hundred and thirty souls
gather ev'ry day in the temple courts

The shepherd king of old
writes the world's first confessional poems

A white dove descending, lighting
upon then rising from the muddy river.

The snakes fled the Em'rald Isle,
when Patrick brought the wild goose of the ancient days.

The Obsidian Sword of Damocles

Descending from regions above,
transparent as the truth,
it's razor's edge
struck close to the heart,
wounding me,
making me bleed.

A Familiar Exposition of Dorian Grey

The shadow of a diseased reflection,
rests, upon his evening eye.

The venom he desires to spew
at his mirror-self, refusing to be
constrained behind clenched teeth
breaks loose, vomiting itself off his tongue.

The Lover of Lilies

The Lover of lilies, and of man,
the wretched creature He came to save.

The Feeder of sparrows and 5000,
He was the Bread of Life,
delivering us from strife eternal.

He romped with animals
and walked with men,
dying to save us was His end.

The Lover of lilies, and of man,
alive now in Heaven, soon He'll come again.

Why We Remember Her

Mid-winter's icy chill
stopped cold at the door
of the angel of despair.

In the hours before
a mid-day London dawn,
the silenced drumbeat of
her heart went unnoticed
by ears turned blue;
poisoned air
filled the self-sealed room.

The Grass on the Other Side

They return ev'ry day to the daily grind,
tired faces and weary feet;
bodies bearing the brunt
of life upon the concrete plains,
harboring jealousy towards the cubical warriors
roaming the wastes of their prefabricated realms,
as those living in neither world,
peer from the outside looking in;
wishing they had it so good.

Sylvia

Sweet sullen soul spent;
seasons of solace sought
and never found.

Storm clouds gathered,
despair darkening behind the eyes,
her inspiration and doom
walking hand in hand.

Gathering Dust

She stopped reading
the letter her first love wrote.

Gathering dust,
it lies neglected on her bookshelf,
the words slowly fading from her heart.

The Reality of a Dream

As if
in a dream,
I felt the swerve's sudden stop.

My mother died that day;
and I, did not.

The World Has Changed

Silent wailing, the banshee passed unheard
with the waning of the moon,
   for the world has changed

Ripped from this mortal coil, a dear one
slips through the veil to the eternal side of time,
   for the world has changed

Standing alone; together,
grave-side companions face the waxing of the sun,
   for the world has changed.

God Sacrifice

Seven words spoken in whispered screams of anguish,
stunned silence shrouds the trembling earth,
sorrow-filled beneath the tears of the weeping sky.

Such was the scene when the price was paid,
in the deal between Father and Son,
and God was sacrificed for man.

The Rising Sun's Sky

When he came into this world,
its second war's end was drawing nigh,
born, as winged man brought the fire,
that burned and cracked the Rising Sun's sky.

Men with Rifles

Men with rifles
are coming in lockstep,
marching with a purpose
down the crowded city street.

Weekend warriors
in uniform blue or grey,
there to honor the fallen,
once was once,
Decoration Day.

Fear the Folly of Fallen Fools

Fear the folly of fallen fools,
those rebels of conscience in the hallowed halls.

With the Devil in the details
and absolute power,
they corrupted absolutely,
forgetting their sacred vow.

Much could be said of their "indiscretions".
But what of we, the fools who follow them?

Olive Garden Confession

My courage; it fled into the night
(while the shadows came, and the shadows ruled),
farther than the fading of the torch light,
and the murmurs of lesser men.

Here was a man who knew our plight,
a king to place our hopes upon.
But he surrendered when it was time to fight,
so, my mind is screaming, questioning why.

Weather Traiku

The grey geese have fled
to fields far away, leaving
white feathers behind.

The sun and clouds war
for blue or grey skies, the winds
say it will be white.

The cherry blossoms
in white, bloom upon the tree,
soon fall to the ground.

Co-worker Relations

The rage in my heart
that makes Banner's "friend" flee,
is when the people at work,
act as if I speak Swahili.

Sages of the Inexpressible

We few, we happy few, *
we band of poets,
sages of the inexpressible,
feeling what the world yearns to feel,
writing what it cannot utter.

As both ballast and balloon,
we anchor the masses to the depths
and lift them to brand new heights,
ensuring they will live another day.

*St. Crispin's Day Speech Henry V Act 4 Scene 3
– William Shakespeare*

The Poet on Stage

Shooting syllables in rapid fire succession,
delivers a sonnet in true spoken word fashion.
The audience in deep appreciation,
thirsty for more rain from his poetic storm,
waits to hear another with much anticipation.

Instead, what they get is a man saying
oo lah lah with increasing jubilation,
'til he rips the microphone and mount
off the stand without hesitation.

End of Poem

End of poem;
a phrase to denote its conclusion
and time to commence your applause.

It also stands in this imperfect world
against the dreaded Shatner pause,
where I tell you "IT IS MY SHIP"
and "set phasers on stun".

So now to bring about this poem's completion,
I hearken to the words at its inception,
and simply say,
end of poem.

Bitter Pill

Dad died.

A fortnight passed
before I heard the news.

After all these years,
I never knew him.

Balance

In defense of the fly
he killed the spider,
ending its web of oppression.

And in gratitude, the flies
(which he thought he was lord of),
did what flies will do,
filling his house with their buzzing,
'til they were more,
than he could get rid of.

Adultery

Gazing,
his eyes linger
upon her nubile form,
hoping she'll tremble,
when she sleeps
with him.

The Gods of Sleep

The gods of sleep come ev'ry night;
breathless, unable to give him rest,
and returning to him in the morn,
he lays upon his vertical bed.

A hand up, a hand up for the fallen,
whom gravity has used its power on,
and there among the forklifts
(that are no respecter of pallets and people)
leaves him lying on the concrete floor.

The King in His Castle

The king in his castle
sits upon the throne,
hours at a time,
reading poetry and playing games,
until his queen comes calling,
to tell him to hurry,
she has to use the bathroom.

That Moment You Beat Your Head Against a Brick Wall to Knock Yourself Out

After five years of his ev'ry advance rebuked
(holding her hand, caressing her cheek),
he stopped
seeing the futility of beating a dead horse;
and she rebuked him again,
for not trying anymore.

A Poem for the End

Here's a poem for the end
and the new year that soon begins.

Waiting in the waning hours
before the old man becomes a child,
we celebrate and remember,
love and laughter, sorrow and tears,
new friends found; old ones lost.

Another journey, once 'round the sun,
fades, slipping into the past.

We face the future, abundant with what
is not new under the sun,
success and failure, joy and sadness,
and as we strive for a better life,
let us dare to be content.

This Empty House

This empty house,
a testament to the failure
of us together,
life in its demands
to move forward; separately,
forces on us heart holes
bigger than this empty house
we're leaving behind.

Her Soul Screamed Medusa

Such an alluring visage,
a feast for the eyes.
She had a tight body,
with curves
in all the right places,
but her soul screamed Medusa.

The day she left,
the nightmares stopped,
and like her,
never came back.

I'll Never Run to You Again

I'll never run to you again
the way I did years before,
when I, as a fool, asked for your hand,
knowing you did not want me.

In the intervening years
so many things have changed,
but your feelings,
they have not,
and they never will.

The Vulgarity Found in the Expression of Human Thought

The vulgarity found
in the expression of human thought
goes much deeper
than the one syllable colloquialisms
coloring our vernacular;
it seeps as rivers of venom,
flowing from hateful hearts
and hateful minds,
rolling itself off the tongue.

An Apathetic Reaction to a Heinous Act, Now Mundane

Another mass shooting,
I drop my head at the news
with a fleeting twinge of passing sorrow,
shock and tears have long since fled,
as the act progresses
from heinous to horrific,
to horrible, to commonplace,
then mundane,
and finally;
meh.

In the Time It Takes

In the time it takes to read this,
another soul lost, taken,
enticed by the cruel claws
of demons desiring their demise.

The ongoing series of despairing days
drives them to the edge of the abyss,
and sometimes
(both knowing and unknowing),
we in the blackness of our hearts,
give them cause to surrender to it.

No Longer Golden

92

A distraction 'round ev'ry corner,
there's something new to hear and see,
ev'ry second of ev'ry day.

We sleep to the sound of t.v. or radio,
pursuing constant stimulation.

Should the crush
of the cessation of sound befall us,
how do we endure?

For the sound of silence is no longer golden,
but deafening.

Tolerance

93

In this season
where societal standards slowly shift,
I'm expected to accept and agree.

Holding to absolutes
and expressing my beliefs publicly to
persuade others,
renders me intolerable
and not to be tolerated.

I Will Laugh Again

I have no brave face to show,
your candle passed
midst a roadside accident,
and though I mourn,
I will laugh again

I have no brave face to show,
your candle passed
silently into the night,
and though I mourn,
I will laugh again.

I have no brave face to show,
your candle passed,
led by demons of despair,
and though I mourn,
I will laugh again.

Libido

I need you
I want you
I love you,
your body is all I seek

I need you
I want you
I love you,
until I meet someone else

Libido is the hallmark of my faithfulness

April Muse

The words flow like water filling a tub,
which is where I meet you
to be both clean and creative.

April muse whispers in my mind
the verse to be committed to paper,
for future generations yet to be.

A Brief Poem on the Subject of Minimalist Poems

Sometimes
it can be said
in the briefest of ways,
and sometimes,
what we really need
is prose.

He Writes of Dawn in Darker Shades

His dark expression upon the page
reflects the beauty of Dawn
at war with the shadows
for the souls of mortal men
who stumble in this season
of always winter.

And with those writing in rainbow hues,
he helps to show the way
of further up and further in,
and points to the lamp post in a wood,
where we are forgetting Christmas.

The Greatest Ship on the Sea

How can any ship
be the greatest on the sea,
when its crew is below deck,
blowing holes in the hull
beneath the water line?

The Basis of Not Having a Romantic Relationship

She is beautiful
and she is distant;
many miles lie between us
(over half the country in fact).

But even more than that,
there is a woman
who already holds my heart,
and I would never give her up,
even for the world.

Her Literary Lover

She falls asleep,
a book for her bed,
dreaming blissful dreams,
there in the arms of her literary lover.

And she's had many in her day,
all poetry and prose in ev'ry genre.

Comfort comes to her on the pages
she reads to herself alone,
more so than any living soul she knows
here on Earth under Heaven.

Atlas is Failing to Hold up the Sky

He cannot do it all,
but still he must
to attend to and provide
for ev'ryone's needs, ev'ryone's desires
as he holds up the sky.

The ever-increasing weight
of all he must do,
shifts from shoulders to back
(there is no one who will share the load).

And when he asks
they help bear the burden,
he is greeted with rage, or "if I must"
dripping from their tongues,
for they are not his slaves,
yet expect him to be theirs.

It's All About Me

When the fog is lifted on my intent
(burned away by the Son),
I am diminished in my pride,
arrogance, broken and laid bare.

For in my skewed backstage view,
it's all about me,
and everyone sees it.

Her Face is in the Winter Sky

Her face is in the winter sky;
I dwell in the trees below.

Gazing down in longing,
she sends eagles soaring high,
to beckon me, encourage me,
to rise,
to join,
to be her lover.

Doppelganger

Hardened in the river of blood baptism,
the warrior unrivaled in war,
fear fills his fearless eyes,
as his familiar face stares back at him
across the field of battle.

Muse for a Minute
(for Asuka)

She was my muse for a minute.
Her performance on the squared stage drew nigh,
inspiring me to craft a few lines of verse
for the world to mull over.

How the Abuse Begins

I long for you to caress my cheek,
but will settle for your backhand,
if that's the only way you'll touch me
because you want to.

Acid Rain

The verbal acid rain
I hear all around me,
falls freely, ev'rywhere I turn,
slowly seeping into my heart and mind,
infecting my tongue.

And when a profane utterance
escapes past my lips,
I'll be nailed to the wall by a world
that curses, the way they breathe.

The Most Dangerous in the World

We are poets,
able to assassinate with similes
and murder you in metaphor.

Anger or upset us
and we could destroy you in verse,
or let you live.

Stolen

Left unguarded,
ripe for the taking,
stolen and lost forever.

For the sake of sleep
he let it linger,
never bothering
to write it down.

Little Glimpses of Glory

Little glimpses of Glory
for the benefit of the damned,
seen ev'rywhere
the Bridegroom's betrothed
wanders over the Earth.

James E. Roéthlein Profile:

James has been writing for 22 years; his work has appeared in Canada, Australia, and the United States. In 2010 and he was nominated for a Pushcart Prize. James is also a regular participant on the internet radio program World Poetry Open Mic.

He currently resides in Middletown Pa. USA where he is a member of the Pa. Civil War re-enactment group, as well as being a servant to his three cats (Bela, Freddy, and Pepper).